A Vision Distorted

MANIFESTED TRUTH * CHILDLIKE TRUTH * TRUE COVENANT FIRM

Jennifer A. Marion

Copyright © 2018 by Jennifer A. Marion

A Vision Distorted
Visit the author's website at www.empoweringvisions05.com
Publisher: Manifested Truth Publishing: www.manifestedtruth.org

Printed in the United States of America.

Edited by Morshe Araujo
ISBN 978-0-578-20285-3

All rights reserved solely by the author. The author guarantees all contents are original and do not infringe upon the legal rights of any other person or work. No part of this book may be reproduced in any form without the permission of the author.

Unless otherwise indicated, all Scripture quotations are taken from the King James Version of the Holy Bible.

Scripture quotations marked (NIV) are taken from THE HOLY BIBLE, NEW INTERNATIONAL VERSION®, NIV®, Copyright © 1973, 1978, 1984 by International Bible Society®. Used by permission of Zondervan. All rights reserved worldwide.

Unless otherwise noted, all word definitions are taken from the Merriam-Webster online dictionary, www.m-w.com.

Dedication

This book is dedicated to every individual who would not allow the devil to distort their vision. You became more than conquerors and trusted in God's plan and purpose for your life. You are victorious! Keep running after God, following your dreams, and fulfilling your purpose.

Prayer

"...After that he put his hands again upon his eyes and made him look up: and he was restored, and saw every man clearly."

Mark 8:25-26

Abba Father, I honor You today as the God of our creation. The God that created us from the dust of the earth and blew the breath of life into our nostrils. The God who provided my life with divine purpose when I was just a mere substance. Before you formed me Father, I was given a calling and ordained for purpose. I am a special representative of God in the world. Do not allow my vision to be distorted by the wickedness or deceitfulness of the enemy. Remove the blinders from my eyes and restore my sight. Lord, allow my vision to be clear to walk out my God-given destiny. In the name of Jesus Christ, I pray, Amen!

"Your Word is a lamp for my feet, a light on my path."

Psalm 119:105

CONTENTS

Introduction 8
Chapter 1: Exposing Your Sins 12
Chapter 2: Take Me as I Am 17
Chapter 3: Vision and Purpose 25
Chapter 4: A Vision Distorted 30
Chapter 5: A Shattered Vision 37
Chapter 6: Spirit of Rejection 42
Chapter 7: Purpose of the Enemy 45
Chapter 8: Set Free 49
Chapter 9: God Changed My Name 61
Chapter 10: Write the Vision, Make it Plain 65
Chapter 11: Walking in My God-given Purpose 68
The Author's Final Words 75
Appendix A: Practical Exercise 78
Appendix B: Cognitive Distortions 86
About the Author 90

My Prayer

God give me vision, so I may see
The work You try to do through me
I need to visualize
The many blessings you want to place before my eyes
Your vision provides purpose and direction
If I continue to follow Your lead, I will learn life lessons
No more looking back, I am focusing on my progression
Anointed for purpose
Destined for greatness
Thanking You God for being so gracious

Jennifer A. Marion

Introduction

This book is about the purpose of God being fulfilled in your life despite the difficulties you will face. Many challenges will be presented to you throughout life. Do not allow those challenges to stop your purpose from being fulfilled. I want to stop right here and tell each one of you, "you were not an accident." I know parents that tell their children this lie. I was given this excuse to explain my conception and birth. I would always say, I might not have been in your plans, but I was in God's plan. Your conception probably was a shock to your parents, but not to God. Please do not allow this excuse to determine your life. Long before we were conceived in our mother's womb, God already determined our calling and purpose to be fulfilled on earth.

Before I was placed in my mother's womb, I was given a God-ordained purpose. God declares in Jeremiah 1:5, "Before I formed you in the womb I knew you, before you were born I set you apart; I appointed you as a prophet to the nations" (NIV). In this passage, God was encouraging Jeremiah to be confident in his call to leadership. Jeremiah was given a purpose from God, but he did not understand the totality of the responsibility. Jeremiah's gifts would allow him to communicate the will of God to the people. Jeremiah was given the ordination and appointment from God to prophesy to the nations. God placed great value and meaning on Jeremiah's life before he was even formed.

God has placed this same responsibility on each of us. An additional Scripture to reference is Psalm 139:15-16, which states, "My frame was not hidden from you when I was made in the secret place, when I was woven together in the depths of the earth. Your eyes saw my unformed body; all the days ordained for me were written in your book before one of them came to be" (NIV). David was declaring God fixed His eyes upon him before being in the womb, before conception. God knew him when he was nothing more than a mere substance. God envisioned our conception, formed us, gave us a meaning for life, and drew out a purposeful plan to be fulfilled. You have a specific purpose and was chosen by God for a divine mission.

Everyone might not be a prophet like Jeremiah, but we have a calling. As you begin to read this book, I want you to understand, you have a purpose. You are not here by chance. God provided the story of your life when you were just a mere substance. That's how much He cares about you. God has called you and ordained you for your assignment. The next time someone murmurs you were an accident, tell them God has a plan for your life, and you are a special representative of Him on earth. You were intricately made by the Father of creation. Do not allow those negative words to take root. Negative words or negative thoughts will make you deny the true significance of your life.

Moses was called by God to deliver the Israelites from Egypt, but he did not understand how significant his life was. Moses told the Lord, "he was not eloquent, slow of speech and of slow tongue." He started making excuses about who God called him to become. God told Moses, "Who hath made man's mouth? Or who maketh the dumb, or deaf, or the seeing, or the blind? Have not I the Lord?" God has given us everything we need to fulfill our purpose. We must trust Him! Stop making excuses on why you feel you are inadequate. Today, I want you to know your life has value and meaning. Walk into your destiny with your head held high on the path God has chosen.

The body of Christ must know and understand there is a constant battle if you desire to walk out your God-given purpose. The enemy doesn't want you to fulfill your purpose. Satan will try to send many distractions your way. I have experienced a lot of difficulties and struggles throughout my life that has created obstacles I had to overcome. I had to find my identity in Christ to understand my life had true meaning.

Throughout this book, I will share my testimonies for you to understand my valley experiences. My valley experiences came to me when I dealt with the struggles of life, but I couldn't find my way out. I will share how I transitioned from my valley experiences to the top of the hill.

Chapter 1

Exposing Your Sins

This book was given to me because of the "Birthing Your Purpose" 2017 Women's Empowerment Conference I hosted in Gulfport, Mississippi. Blessings! When God dropped this book into my spirit, I was excited to see which angle He was going to lead me. There were so many phenomenal speakers ministering at this conference. I sought God to see what message I would deliver to help empower the women. Before I went to sleep for that night, I asked Him, "What makes people stop walking towards their God-given purpose?" When I awaken from the dream, I heard the Lord say, "A Vision Distorted." Originally, I started writing a lesson to teach on "*a distorted vision,*" but God changed my focus to "*a vision distorted.*" It does not mean the title was wrong, God wanted me to deliver the message differently.

Distortion means an act of twisting or altering something out of its true, natural, or original state. A distorted vision is one that has been twisted or altered to something that is not true. A vision distorted means God provided the vision for the person, but an action (person, place, or thing) twisted or altered it from its true, natural, or original state. It is an impairment in your ability to see clearly. When I began to prepare for this message through research and studying, God stopped me. God instructed me to tell the women attending the conference how my vision was distorted. He wanted me to share what stopped me from walking in my purpose. I pondered this request from the Lord.

God wanted me to disclose my sins, disappointments, and problems that kept me from serving Him. Really? Well, we all know I obeyed God's request, and followed His direction. Sometimes, the hardest thing to do is be transparent in front of others. I have shared some parts of my testimony to people, but God wanted to expose my whole life during a conference. I quickly decided it would be important for me to buy a mirror for this life lesson. This would be a session for the women of the conference, and a life lesson for me. I acquired a mirror through a friend of mine and decided it was too beautiful to write on, but God gave me a mission and I had to fulfill it. As I looked in this mirror, I saw the beautiful creation God made in me.

Throughout life, I viewed myself as a dusty, cracked gemstone, and God turned me into a precious ruby. I began to write the things that prevented me from living out my God-given purpose. I wrote things I had shared with a few people, but I was tired of hiding it from others. We hide our sins out of shame, guilt, disappointment, and embarrassment. It's crazy how we will commit an act but be reluctant to share the story with others. Our sins are only visible to us, and we wear the scars daily. Some people have scars hidden so deep, they'd rather go to their grave with the act, than receive deliverance and healing. When a person hides from their sins, the sin still has power over them.

God's love toward us convicts, not condemns. A conviction makes you aware of the sin and results in you confessing or repenting. Conviction is the work of the Holy Spirit. Condemnation is to pass judgment, punishment or a verdict on someone. Condemnation is the work of the devil. He doesn't want you to be changed. God wants us to recognize our sin, repent, and be changed. I had to face my fears and tell the people God changed me. When I walked into that sanctuary, I asked God to decrease my flesh, and increase His Spirit who lived within me. I trusted God, and He delivered my message.

Some things I wrote on the mirror included: fornicator, adulterer, cheater, liar, prideful, fly mouth, manipulator, controller, gossiper, murderer, alcoholic, disobedience, rebellion, theft, selfishness, and unforgiveness. These terms among others described me and the lifestyle I chose to live. The conference's attendees learned how important it was to recognize their sins to change their life. I will share a little of my testimony in the next chapter. I pray being transparent and open about my life will increase your understanding and promote change in you. Never hide your testimony because someone is waiting to hear there is a way out of their mess.

People overcome by the blood of the lamb, and the power of our testimonies. The blood of the lamb is the only thing that can cleanse people from their sins. It's through the power of the blood of Jesus Christ that we have liberty and victory. Our testimonies have the power to deliver and set captives free. The testimony demonstrates the power of Christ working in our lives. A testimony encourages others dealing with the same issues they can overcome if they believe in the power of Christ.

Questions for Reflection

1) What sins are you hiding that God wants to expose?

2) Have you presented these sins to God to seek forgiveness? If not, why?

3) Have you allowed this sin to distort your vision? Why?

4) Will you become a walking testimony for others?

Chapter 2
Take Me as I Am

My vision was distorted from seeing God clearly because I focused on my sins more than I focused on God. My personal testimonies in this book are shared so every person reading can understand how God cleansed me of my sins and changed my name. I am going to be transparent and share some of the sins that was written on that mirror that day. I started early focusing on my purpose as a young girl. I have always been a smart individual who wanted more in life. I was raised in the church since it was located right across the street from my grandparents' house.

I was like everyone that was raised in the church by great parents, grandparents, aunts, and mothers of the community.

I knew what it meant to live a good life, be obedient to my elders, and act like a young lady. I accepted the Lord as my personal Savior at twelve, and I was eager to serve Him. But I never expected life to be so hard. Even though all these great things were happening in my life, I still wanted more. I truly believe when you start looking for the wrong things in life, it will definitely find you. I had friends, but I wanted to be liked and accepted by others. I wanted to be a popular girl that everyone looked up to, and for the most part I was. During my high school years, I allowed peer pressure to transform me. I began to lie, steal, and have sex as a teenager. I was performing acts that some adults had not experienced.

Every Friday night I looked forward to hanging out with my friends and getting wasted by using drugs and alcohol. We would hang out in clubs using fake identification and thought instant gratification was what we needed at that age. In reality, what I needed was the love of God. I was living a life of self-destruction, and I did not even know it.

God knew the direction my life was headed, and He had to wake me up to save my life. Believe me, God's plan was already in motion. At the age of eighteen, I was a senior in high school who found out I was pregnant. I was so hurt I didn't know what to do. I didn't want my family to know, especially my grandmother. I believed she would be hurt and disown me. I contemplated having an abortion, but I could not go through with it. I wanted to give the baby up for adoption, but I could not imagine birthing a child and giving it away. I was two months from graduating from high school, and my actions left me with the tough responsibility of having a child. I enjoyed hanging out, drinking and smoking, and having sex. I did not want this responsibility.

I was a child myself preparing to bring a child into the world. I attended college in Alabama; but ended up dropping out after one month. I was an emotional wreck and being pregnant did not help. High levels of stress almost made me have my child early. I had to find peace to ease my mind. My son came into this world December 28, 2001. When I saw that handsome face of his, I knew I would have to change my life. I alone had to provide for and protect my son. I could not focus on his father being a part of his life. I was not respected by my son's father, nor did he care.

I was fighting over a person who was sleeping with other women. One of his friends had a child a couple of months after I had given birth. He caused a pain and suffering in my life so bad, I had contemplated how I could get away with killing him. I was hurt and rejected. That was not the life I wanted for me or my new child. He deserved more even if I could not provide it for him at the time.

I stopped drinking, smoking, and I decided to be a good mother. My oldest sister talked me into joining the military to get away from Mississippi. She knew my life had purpose, but I had to move away to see what God had for me. I was worried about joining because I did not want to leave my newborn. He was two months old. My sister, mother, and grandmother assured me they would take great care of him. I decided that day to join the military, and I never looked back. When I first joined the military, I was focusing on making a better life for my child.

My son became my world, and dating was not one of my interests. Over time, I met someone who I became attached to romantically. He was a great person, and he was a phenomenal father figure for my son. We started dating, and I became pregnant. I did not want to be a single parent of two kids. So, I married him and had my second child, which was a little girl. Finally, I felt like my life was turning around for good. I was so happy to have a family. The spirit of rejection showed itself again in my life, but this time I allowed the spirit of rebellion to take root.

I want to talk about some issues I dealt with in my first marriage, but I do not want anyone to think I am bashing him. He continues to be a good father to my daughter, and I appreciate that. He did not understand what it meant to be a provider and protector of his family. My husband at that time did not realize we were enough for him. He had infidelity issues, hung out with his friends more than us, and could not stop smoking weed. He ended up losing his job in the military because of his disobedience. I became pregnant with my third child, but we could not afford it.

The Roller Coaster Effect

I did not want to have another child by a man that did not provide for me. We decided to have an abortion. I can tell anyone reading this that having an abortion was one of the hardest things I have ever done. I prevented a life from entering this world because I was selfish. I became a murderer. Medical science has provided substantial evidence and research that when women conceive, there is an instant formulation of major organs. This means there is a formulation of a human being. That is why having an abortion is considered a murder. After having an abortion, I felt so lost. I was angry, depressed, lonely and worthless.

I started seeking revenge for my husband's infidelity. I am not blaming him for my mistakes because I had to learn to take ownership of my own faults. But, I found myself in a relationship with a married man to ease the pain I experienced in my marriage. During that marital affair, I started drinking and hanging out with my friends in the club. I was in the military, a professional organization, drinking and fighting in the club. Not only that, I could leave the club and go straight to church with a hangover.

I thought what I was doing was acceptable in the sight of the Lord, but I was wrong. I can tell you, even amid my trials, I never steered away from God or the church. My family trained me up in the ways of the Lord. When you are trained in God, you know where to turn when you are faced with the issues of life. The problem was I did not trust Him enough to help me. My husband found out about the relationship I was in, and that caused some unnecessary drama. I ended the extramarital relationship, but I began to fall out of love with my husband.

We decided to attend marriage counseling, but after two sessions my husband stopped going. Generally, black men do not embrace counseling, or they will not seek help from others when issues arise. There is a large body of research that shows men are less likely than women to seek any form of support to include counseling. The reason black men don't want to seek counseling is due to stigma and judgment, concerns about therapy and the treatment process, cost of the treatment, and lack of insurance coverage.

In my ex-husbands case, it was the stigmatism that people who attend counseling are crazy. He would rather hang out with his friends than fix our relationship problems. My life continued a downward spiral, and I saw no way of escape. After a few more months, the military moved us to Virginia. During school, I found out I was pregnant again by a man I was falling out of love with. My selfishness and the hate I had within my heart for my husband convinced me to have another abortion.

I was broken, and I needed someone to help me get through. I called my father, and he shared some great words of wisdom with me. He assured me I did not have to go through life alone. I needed that encouragement from him to finish the military school. Luckily, I finished school, and we moved to Hawaii to work on our relationship. In truth, the relationship only got worse. After my arrival to Hawaii, I deployed for the first time to Iraq. I was working in an occupation that took me thousands of miles away from my children, and I was losing my husband.

There are plenty of reasons our marriage did not work. Both of us were young and did not put forth the effort to make it work. Life was not what our parents tried to make it seem. My grandparents were married about fifty-eight years before they passed away. I thought I would be a princess that would be carried away by her prince, but I was wrong. My life was a struggle. Even during my trials, God provided me hope. I have always been a dreamer, and most of my dreams would come true.

One night, I had a dream about a particular guy in my unit. It wasn't a sexual dream, but for some reason I could not get him out of my mind. I would dream every night about this man. I started seeing him everywhere I went. I didn't know if it was a coincidence or not. Next thing you know, we bumped into each other and became friends. When people are broken, God will bring them together to comfort one another. It was through this friendship that I started learning what love truly meant.

When I returned to Hawaii, I filed for divorce. I realized I had done so much wrong in my life, and I finally had a glimpse of hope. I wanted to enjoy life and become a great example for my two children, who desired my very best, and I believed this guy was the answer. I could not believe how compatible we were. I know this might sound silly, but he completed me. Where I was weak, he was strong. We complemented each other very well. After both of us were free from our marriages, we decided to take a chance and become a couple. Being in a relationship was hard since we brought all the burdens we carried from life and other relationships with us. We had to learn to love ourselves first, and then love each other.

I endured many struggles, but this chapter would encompass the whole book if I told every single detail. There were so many things that happened to me from my so-called friends, family, and job. I had to be transparent enough to allow you to see the different things that stopped me from walking in my purpose. Why did I entitle this chapter, "Take Me as I Am?" The things written in this chapter were my shortfalls. I am a human being made up of flesh. I wanted to follow God, but my flesh was weak.

I have failed numerous times, and I have lived a life of sin. In my mind, I believed if God wanted me to serve Him, He would have to take me as the sinner I was. These were the sins I saw daily when I looked into the mirror. I did not see the person God knew I would become. I saw my imperfections. I knew I was messed up, and I relied on God to fix me. God had to provide me with a vision for me to understand my purpose. I believe the vision God gave me came through those dreams I started experiencing.

Questions for Reflection

1) What does "Take Me as I Am" mean to you?

2) Do you allow other people, places, or things to place a barrier between your relationship with God?

3) What hope has God given you?

4) What vision has God provided you to live out your purpose?

Chapter 3
Vision and Purpose

God has great things and plans in store for us. God's plan is the vision; the blueprint for our life's journey. Everyone has their own vision that contributes to God's inclusive plan. Having vision means you have the ability to see, think or plan the future with your imagination or wisdom. This vision could be a mental image or a supernatural illustration that is given through dreams or a trance. Just as our eyes provide vision for our physical bodies, God provides vision for our spiritual bodies. Godly vision provides an individual with direction and purpose. God communicates His will through visions. There are plenty of stories throughout the *Bible* where God provided seers and prophet's vision to restore and revive the people. When there is an absence of vision, the people decline.

The Word of God states, "Without vision, the people perish" (Proverbs 29:18). When people are not provided vision from God for their steps to be ordered, they lack focus and direction. I had to learn God can provide the vision, and yet we still lack. This is because we still must be disciplined to follow God's lead to see the vision fulfilled. Joseph did not get put in charge of the whole land of Egypt overnight. God gave him a vision, and he had faith it would come to pass. God communicated His will and way to Joseph, but He did not provide the details. Joseph was betrayed, lied on, and left behind, but he still held onto the vision. Despite Joseph's circumstances and the things, he had to endure, he still believed in God.

I worked with different types of engineers in the Army. What I learned from them was the process it took to get a building created. They would receive a request from a leader for the project. The leader would give them the vision he had for the project. The engineer would have to research, study, and survey the area before any action could be taken. Next, they would have to receive a budget, find the right materials for the project, get the proper codes to be used, and draft a strategic plan. The plan was a step-by-step guide. After all that information was received, they would produce a blueprint and the job would start, if approved. This was an intricate process that took anywhere from one to five years.

Every detail had to be researched and implemented. We must perform the same type of actions for God's plan. When we are given vision, we must research the Word of God to validate the source. Next, we need to write the vision down in explicit detail to provide directions to the destination. We need to see what we need for the vision to come to pass. Some visions need plenty of prayer, meditation on the Word of God, praise and worship, and revelation. Every intricate detail needs to be worked out before laying a foundation on the ground. It is your vision that will define your purpose.

A person's vision aligns perfectly with their purpose. God created every living thing with purpose. The trees that grow all around us have a purpose. Every science class throughout America teaches the importance of trees. According to the Environmental Thinker (2009), trees produce oxygen, sequesters carbon, prevent erosion, distill water, provide habitats for hundreds of species, accrue solar energy, make complex sugars and foods, create micro climates, and self-replicates. Some trees produce fruit for us to eat. The point is God created trees to have a purpose, and He created you for a specific purpose.

God has given every one of us a purpose before we were formed in our mother's womb. The message of Samson's purpose was given by the angel of the Lord to his mother. She received a detailed word from God. She was given instructions on what to eat and drink during the pregnancy. The mother of Samson was given a vision of her future child. She learned her son's purpose before he was even formed in the womb, and that was to deliver the Israelites out of the hands of the Philistines. The angel did not tell her the things her son would endure. Samson had vision, but he would have to walk out his God-given purpose. He was not given a blueprint from God to defeat the Philistines. He had to trust God and have faith in His plan. Even though Samson made mistakes, he still yielded to God's great purpose for his life.

When we believe in the vision God has given us, no distraction, obstacle, discouragement, or disappointment will stop us from fulfilling it. Some people get overwhelmed because they want their vision to happen immediately. Be patient and wait on God's timing for your vision to come to pass. Allow the vision to manifest in your spirit. We must exercise our faith when waiting on a vision to come to pass. Faith is the substance of things hope for, the evidence of things not seen. A way to increase your faith is by reading the Word of God. The more you feed on the Word of God, the more your faith will grow. Take slow and steady steps of faith towards your vision to fulfill your purpose. If not, the devil will try to distort your vision.

Questions for Reflection

1) What vision has God given you to fulfill your purpose?

2) What steps do you need to take to start the process? Do you appreciate the small steps taken? Why?

3) Are you a person of patience? How can you increase your faith in God?

Chapter 4
A Vision Distorted

As a little girl, I had a vision to become a successful woman with a husband and children. Even though that was not the vision God provided, I still had a starting point. I allowed the issues and stressors of life to distract me. I carried my sins with me instead of releasing them to the Lord. As I looked in the mirror every day, the devil made me see my imperfections. In that mirror, I did not see the person I was to become, I saw my sins. I saw the things keeping me from my God-given purpose. Later, in my life, I was given a supernatural vision, but I could not get past my wrongdoings. I started believing God could not change me because my sins were too great.

How could I be a prophet to the nations when I was a sinner? How could I prophesy to God's people knowing the things I did in my life? How could I teach the nations when people knew the things I had done? How could I save souls? These are the questions among others that I asked myself. I was looking in a mirror, but I could not clearly see because the devil was blocking my view. It's like being in a dark room in your home. You know where everything is in the home, but you cannot see clearly to get to the light. You know if the light was turned on you could see. When the light is off, you are left in that dark place bumping into stuff. No matter how familiar you are with the room, the darkness still obstructs your vision.

When a person has a physical impairment or a distorted vision, the object they see does not appear straight. The object is bent, crooked, or wavy. Their view of the object can change their perception. That person cannot imagine how they want their lives to become. It does not matter which angle the image is viewed, it will still produce an inaccuracy. The most common cause of a distorted vision is an error. When referring to your physical eyesight, the error could be a variety of things such as a disease, disorder or eye condition. A distorted vision can vary depending on the underlying cause. In my life, the things which caused the distortion were my emotions, opportunity, and people.

Emotional

People must endure trials in their lives that cause emotional problems. For instance, I had bad relationships that changed me, a child at a young age, a grandmother who passed away, two abortions, a divorce, and a nephew that committed suicide. These are a few things that distorted my vision. The first person we blame when our lives are turned upside down is God. How could I serve a God that would allow these things to happen to a good person? I never focused on the things I did to create some of these situations. I had to place the blame on someone else. I did not want to accept ownership of my problems. I went through life telling people I was "ok!" It was a lie, but I felt good telling it. When I began to tell people I was ok, my mind began to believe the lie as well.

The mind is a powerful thing. It can be viewed as a defense mechanism for our body, wired to protect us by selecting and interpreting evidence to support the notion we are "ok." Our minds have the ability to ignore the bad things occurring, while emphasizing the good to increase our hope and reduce anxiety. We work so hard to believe we are fine, despite the things going on in our lives that declare otherwise. We would rather go to the grave with fabrication than tell someone we need help. Our thinking is a result of our perception, judgment, experience, and bias. The brain can distort our reality by increasing our self-esteem.

When our thinking becomes twisted, our vision is distorted. There is a complete list of common forms of distorted thinking. I wish I could review each one to give you a better idea, but I wanted to focus on the one that altered my vision. In your spare time, research the list of cognitive distortions I have attached in the appendix. Distorted thinking can affect a person's life and produce negative distortions of a person's reality. I was allowing a cognitive distortion to take me from my purpose. My mind convinced me of something that was not true, and I began to believe it. I could not be the person the Lord could use because I had a distorted thought process.

Opportunity

I can remember working hard to get promoted in the Army so more opportunities could present themselves. To attain the next rank and be ahead of my peers, I attended every course required. I never settled for less.

I was focusing on increasing my pay to provide for my family. We need to understand some opportunities come to distort our vision. People attend the right universities to become a professional and receive the certifications that will prepare them for the job. When the opportunity presents itself for us to advance, we move on without seeking God.

Some people move themselves out of the will of God due to their lack of finances. I know people who have moved from the East Coast to the West Coast for an opportunity due to an increase in their finances. They never sought God, only their own personal desires. When opportunities become more important than God, our vision is distorted. Nothing can exalt itself above God.

Let me explain how an opportunity can distort your vision. You begin working at a new organization and realize you are not able to attend Bible Study anymore. The first couple of times is fine, but then you notice you're working late every week. You think there is nothing wrong with working on those nights because you still attend Sunday morning worship.

Well, a promotion presents itself, and you have to pull extra shifts to be recognized. You decide to work on Sundays and get the extra work completed. Your mind tells your body, "we'll still read and meditate on God's Word." You slowly become too distracted due to the opportunity, and your vision becomes distorted of what God desires of you. Not to mention, your job can become an idol if you're not careful. Ultimately, opportunities can distort a person's vision, and those same opportunities can jeopardize your relationship with God.

People

I believe there have been some people in my life who unintentionally were sent to distort my vision. I did not see the spiritual entity that was controlling the individual. I was focused on the things the person did to me. I had to learn my ex-husband could not be a good husband because he was never taught how to be a good man. He did not know what it meant to love or be loved. He also had some issues from his childhood he needed to resolve, but he continued to tell himself everything was ok. It became a cycle of "hurt people hurt people." I was hurt due to his actions, and I allowed my hurt to make me sin against God.

I went to church most of the time, but I did not want to change my ways. I could not see the vision God had for my life. People will put you in a place where you see God, but He is not your main focus. Imagine being a woman that works hard to provide for her husband and children. She works, studies hard to get a degree, cooks and cleans for her husband, and is a nurturer to her children. She has a good life and wonderful family. Her family always makes sure to put God first. Her husband gets laid off, and she is the provider for the family. He cannot find another job, and he begins to drink to cope.

His drinking stops him from attending church because he does not want to be judged. Next thing you know, he gets so angry with his wife one night, and he hits her. This cycle of drinking, anger, and hitting becomes normal. She cannot talk to her friends. They will not understand. She begins to rationalize the behavior is alright because her husband is dealing with life. She stops attending church since they will see the bruises and begin to ask questions. She begins to sulk in her depression and blames God for her husband's actions. She cannot see any good in her life because of her circumstances. Her vision which was once clear, has become very distorted.

This might be a made-up story, but this is reality for some people. Their image of themselves is distorted due to someone else's actions. They do not have the faith needed to trust in God. They have allowed people (significant others, family, and friends) to detour them from reaching their destiny. The truth is, there are people in this world who do not want you to be successful. The problem is, some of us do not know how to recognize those types of people. I have dealt with family members and friends that have caused me some pain and suffering.

I remember being so hurt, I could not hear clearly from God. I questioned God about this issue, as if He sent the person to destroy me. We must be careful of the company we keep, and the people we allow in our lives. Everyone does not have your back as you would wish. Just because someone is your family does not mean they have your best interest at heart. Learn how to differentiate between godly acquaintances and the devil's helpers.

Questions for Reflection

1) What emotional problem has occurred that distorted your vision?

2) What opportunity have you allowed to exalt itself above God? What opportunity has taken you out of the will of God?

3) What type of people have you given access into your life that were sent by the enemy?

4) How can you recover from these things?

Chapter 5
A Shattered Vision

As we were returning from a recent women's conference, my daughter, being careless, placed the distorted mirror in the back of my sports utility vehicle with heavier objects on top of it. She was in a rush and didn't pay attention to her actions. During the drive home, the mirror was accidently shattered. I was a little upset, but my husband looked at me and said, "the vision is not distorted any longer, it is shattered." It amazed me how quickly my distorted vision could become shattered.

If we're not careful, our distorted vision can become isolated, unfinished, or incomplete due to our carelessness. I looked at the mirror, and it was broken into many pieces. A shattered vision produces a different image, which is broken into many pieces, and it takes someone with skill to put the pieces back together. You have an idea of how the pieces should be arranged or fit, but something stops you from completing the task.

A shattered vision will make you look at the big problem without focusing on the solution. You know there is a problem, but you cannot see God through it. It is in our brokenness that good and evil meet. On one side God is reaching for our hands to help, and on the other side the devil is ready to manipulate and control our minds. It is a constant battle where the mind continually plays tricks on you. A person's mind will convince you the cracks cannot be filled, the broken pieces cannot be restored, and there is no way out. The mind will convince you despair, discouragement, emptiness, lack, loss and failure reside in those broken places.

I have met people who knew they were called by God for a purpose. I knew a person who would provide details on how great his life was, and how he was ministering at a young age. He would share his many possibilities. This person had no family, children, or job. When you saw him, he was hanging out on the corner drinking beer and smoking cigarettes. What went wrong? The answer is always, "life." They let the weight of the world bring them down.

When you're knocked down, it's hard to find strength to get up. The only person who can fill those broken places and give you strength is God. A shattered vision shouldn't stop you from moving forward, it should teach you to look to God to put the pieces back together. The one thing I had to teach this person was God still wanted his purpose to be fulfilled. He was still living, so God was waiting on him. I've learned on this journey called life that God will never leave us or forsake us.

God will wait on us to need Him. God wants us to look to Him in all things, especially in moments where we feel hopeless. Sometimes, we look in the wrong direction to people who engage in certain activities that are not godly. We allow those people to encourage us through drugs and alcohol to make us feel good. You will feel better for a moment, but you will have to continuously search for a feeling. The feeling is not what you need to focus on, it is the problem. During the conference, I provided a message of empowerment. The message to empower focused on the fruit of the problem, the root of the problem, and the seed that was planted.

Message to Empower

The fruit of the problem is the behavior a person displays. When looking at a fruit tree, you know what type of fruit is growing by its appearance. If the tree is producing good fruit, it will be healthy and continue to produce. If the tree is not producing fruit, it will slowly wither away. Someone with an alcohol addiction will exhibit behaviors that describes their addiction. The person will have moments of drunkenness and possible anger. The behavior the person exhibits is the fruit of the problem. The type of problem the person has, which in this case is alcoholism, is the root of the problem.

Alcoholism is an illness that makes people suffer through their desire of wanting to drink. An alcoholic is obsessed with alcohol, and they cannot control their consumption. Looking at a tree, you cannot determine the roots because they are hidden. It is through the person's behaviors you realize there is a problem. The root is the object (problem) that needs to be addressed. The person needs the root to be exposed. Going a little beyond the fruit and root of the problem, you will see what type of seed was planted into this person's life that took them away from their purpose.

In this case, the man started drinking to control his stress. When he was younger, his father left the household and the man had to start providing for his mother and siblings. He learned over the years that drinking alleviated the negative feelings he experienced. As a teenager, he did not want to become an adult before his time and support the household. He wanted to play outside with his friends. His life was taken from him, and he had to learn how to be a man. The seed was planted in his life through an absent father among other reasons. He took on a responsibility that was too big for him to handle. The only way he could receive healing and restoration from his problem was to connect to the source.

      He could not release his problem to God because there was a disconnection. A lightbulb cannot work if it is not connected to the power source. When you experience life difficulties and problems, give it to God. We have a source to resolve our problems, we just have to use Him. There is no problem that is too big for God. He can bring us out of our dark places and into the light. Don't allow your vision to remain shattered. Let God put each piece back together, no matter the difficulties.

Questions for Reflection

1) What has shattered your vision? What does the broken pieces represent?

2) Are you trusting God to put the pieces back together?

3) Can you identify the problem you are faced with? What is the fruit of the problem? What is the root of the problem? How was the seed planted?

Chapter 6
Spirit of Rejection

Being told I was an accident as a child or I was never supposed to be born put me in a place of rejection. I didn't feel like I was wanted or accepted in my family. I'm not saying this to hurt anyone's feelings. I'm expressing how I feel. Sometimes we communicate the simplest things to our children and don't realize the consequences of what we have spoken over their lives. I believe my rejection started before I was born. It occurred while I was in the womb. It's very important to recognize when the spirit of rejection started. It will help us determine what we believe about ourselves isn't true.

Rejection can happen after conception. If I wasn't a planned birth and it happened unexpectedly, my parents could've allowed the spirit of rejection entrance into my life. There could have been feelings of shock or disdain. Yes, they decided not to get rid of me, but my birth probably caused an interruption in their lives. A mother can transmit her feelings, attitudes, behaviors and words to the baby while in the womb. A child can sense when they are not accepted. I knew I wasn't an accident, but I allowed myself to suffer inwardly from being rejected.

The feelings I internalized would soon be externalized through my feelings, behaviors, and attitudes. When the spirit of rejection is active in a person's life, other spirits can be given access to torment you. Rejection might be the root cause of your issues, but rebellion, anger, bitterness, resentment, and other things can emerge. Some people begin to act out due to their rejection. For instance, if a child was sexually abused by the opposite sex, they might be reluctant to relate to that person. They could become promiscuous or exhibit homosexual behavior.

The spirit of rejection can cause your vision to be distorted and take you from your purpose. In my case of rejection, I continued to allow that spirit to be relevant in my life. Throughout life, I was rejected in my relationships with friends, family, and people. I felt abandoned due to the death of my loved ones, and I allowed negative words to define me. I started acting out in negative ways due to the pain I felt. I have had issues with being a perfectionist, people-pleaser, aggressive, person who pushes people away, and jealous. Everyone will not experience many scars or deep wounds because of rejection.

God has built some of us to be resilient, but some people will experience serious damage and need help. Rejection can cause physical, psychological, emotional, and mental problems. It doesn't matter if you are the cause of the rejection or there was a misunderstanding, you could be affected. Sometimes the rejection can be so deeply rooted that we must take necessary steps to be set free. I'm not all the way healed from rejection, but I'm trusting God for deliverance. I know man might have rejected me, but God accepted me. He chose me to walk out my God-given purpose. I will not allow the spirit of rejection to stop me from fulfilling my destiny.

Questions for Reflection

1) Do you believe the spirit of rejection is operating in your life? If so, how and why?

2) How has the spirit of rejection tried to destroy you? Was it because of you or others?

3) What does it mean for you to be wanted or accepted? How has God accepted you despite your life experiences?

Chapter 7
Purpose of the Enemy

I want to talk about the devil in this section, I don't want to give him too much credit. He likes the attention and fame, and I will not give him more recognition than he deserves. So, I will keep it short. The problem is we have given the devil too much credit. We believe everything bad that happens in our life is of the devil. When we acknowledge him for something he has not done, he gets credit. Satan cannot perform any action in our lives without the permission of God. How do I know this? Satan had to ask God permission to have access in the life of Job.

Satan told God to take the hedge of protection from around Job. God complied with the request, but with specific instructions. God told Satan he could not take Job's life. The devil comes "to steal, kill, and destroy." He is not a life giver, he is a life taker. The devil will use whatever tool he can to stop you from fulfilling God's purpose. Remember this is a being who wanted to receive more glory than God. His pride got him and a third of the angels kicked out of heaven. Satan does not want you to inherit the Kingdom of God.

He would rather you perform evil, sinful acts, than serve God. He convinced me I was not worthy enough to reap the harvest God promised me. I allowed my past failures and mistakes to define my life. I decided all the wrong things happening in my life were supposed to happen, like I deserved it. I was not living for God. I was living a life of sin for the devil. That's why it is very important not to be ignorant of the devil's schemes. People believe he is powerless, but that is not true. He has power, but he needs permission to interfere in our lives.

Satan is a serpent which can easily camouflage himself from the human eye. The serpent disguises itself to attack the prey. They hide in plain sight unbeknownst to us. If we do not look closely, it will advance and attack with a deadly bite. Satan opposes everything of God and His people. He is an adversary seeking people to perform his acts. When the devil is in control of a person's life, he wants them to perform his will. Their character and conduct resemble that of their master. Satan will use any willing vessel to perform his will by orchestrating opposition through his servants.

Since you are carrying the glory of God within you, Satan wants to stop you from fulfilling your destiny. God and Satan are contending for you. Satan wants dominion over your life. We have been given an assignment from God, but the devil has an assignment against you as well. There was a demonic assignment placed upon your life while you were in your mother's womb.

Satan uses his demonic powers in the kingdom of darkness to help establish a plan. Ephesians 6:12 informs the body of Christ that Satan has a kingdom of darkness which uses strategies and methods to control, deceive, and harm people. "For we wrestle not against flesh and blood, but against principalities, against powers, against the rulers of the darkness of this world, against spiritual wickedness in high places." The entities we fight against in the kingdom of darkness are unseen.

Satan knows if he can convince God's people to rebel against Him and the Word of God, his mission is successful. The battle that we fight against Satan is very real. Satan is a roaring lion that walks over the earth, seeking whom he can devour. He wants to use us up, suck the life out of us, and destroy us. Be sober and vigilant because you will be faced with opposition. You should expect opposition if you follow Jesus Christ.

Be prepared with methods and strategies to fight this spiritual battle against Satan. If you are not prepared for battle, you will lose the war. Your weapons of warfare cannot be carnal. We should understand our struggle in this world is not against flesh and blood, it is against rulers, authorities, powers of this dark world, and spiritual forces of evil in heavenly realms.

Satan and his minions are fighting us in a spiritual battle and we must learn to fight back. We are battling within ourselves to choose between good and evil. He enters your life in the area you have not fully submitted to God. The devil's purpose is to stop you from fulfilling God's promises. It is time to fight back. Equip yourself with the whole armor of God daily and continue to watch and pray. When we fight back, we receive help from the Lord. The only person who can help us fulfill our promises by giving us new life is Jesus.

Questions for Reflection

1) Do you understand the purpose of the enemy?

2) What assignments are noticeable that Satan has placed on your life? What is Satan's purpose for your life?

3) Will you fight back, or will you give up? What methods or strategies have you prepared for the battle?

Chapter 8
Set Free

Satan had an assignment on my life, but God had to cleanse me of my impurities to change my name. God had to give me a new life in Christ. Salvation is the process of being saved by grace through faith. It is a gift from God (Ephesians 2:8). Having faith in Christ allows your soul access to being delivered from sin and its consequences. Sin in this nature is referring to the sin that Adam allowed to enter the world. The wages of sin are death (spiritual), but the gift (Jesus Christ-salvation) of God is eternal life (Romans 6:23). Salvation keeps us from experiencing the wrath of God, and we receive eternal reward for spiritual deliverance.

In Acts 16:30-31, Paul explained to the Philippian jailer what he needed to do to receive salvation. Paul told him to confess with his mouth, believe in his heart, and he would be saved. The jailer performed those actions, received the gift of salvation, and was baptized. In these passages, Paul was referring to an eternal reward. On that day, the jailer and his household were saved due to his faith. They were saved for God's purpose and grace through Christ Jesus. The problem that emerges is people believe once they are saved, the work for the Kingdom of God stops.

As stated earlier, I received the gift of salvation around the age of twelve. I never learned the importance of receiving God's gift. I decided to continue in sin willfully. It does not mean my salvation was revoked because Paul stated in Romans 7:20, "Now if I do that I would not, it is no more I that do it, but sin that dwelleth in me." It meant I wrestled with sin and did not realize conforming to the image of God was a process. No one will change overnight. We will endure and go through the process every day of our lives.

This process is referred to as sanctification. When something is sanctified, it is set apart for the purposes of God. It means to become holy. The Word of God provides the understanding (truth) we need to become pure, holy unto God. God provides us sanctification to enable us to spiritually mature and progress in Him. The more we become obedient to God, the more He grows us. Our character and actions resemble that of Christ. The blood of Christ sets us free from every sin. The problem is we continue to sin because we are made up of flesh. Remember, we are made up of body, spirit and soul.

1 Thessalonians 5:23 states, "I pray God your whole spirit and soul and body be preserved blameless unto the coming of our Lord Jesus Christ." A battle occurs every day between your spirit and flesh. You must decide to walk after your spirit or flesh. The blessing is if you walk after the Spirit of God, you will be led by the Spirit of God. I did not understand that concept, so I willfully chose to sin. I became drawn away by my own desires and lusts (James 1:14-15). Having unprotected sex in

the natural does not stop you from conceiving and giving birth to a child. If we continue to allow our fleshly desires to be fed, it will conceive and give birth to sin. Sin brings death.

God gives us free will or freedom of choice. It is up to us to choose a life of sanctification. I was responsible for my actions, and I was held accountable for the choices I made. I did not understand the sins I committed throughout my life would harm me in my future. I was preaching in the pulpit, teaching the Gospel of Jesus Christ, prophesying, speaking in tongues, and operating in deliverance for others. Through my disobedience to God, I allowed gates, doors or windows of darkness to be opened in my life.

I had given the devil a foothold in my life as Paul referred to in Ephesians 4:27. Paul was instructing believers to not allow anger to become unresolved. Being angry is not the issue or sin. Anger can open the door to sin if it is unresolved. I allowed Satan free access in my life to oppress or harass me. We have become so ignorant of Satan's devices that we do not understand half of the things we do daily allows him access in our life. People go to palm readers, cast spells, watch and listen to things that are demonic in nature, curse others, and operate in disobedience.

There are so many ways Satan can infiltrate the lives of believers and unbelievers. I did not resist sin, so I became a slave to it. If you do not resolve or repent of your sin, you will give the devil a foothold in your life. I did repent of some sins, but I was unaware of a lot of other things. In my case, I had several spirits attacking me trying to stop me from fulfilling God's purpose for my life. I am not going to provide detail of every one of my sins, but I will provide some insight.

I had given a python spirit access to suck the breath of life out of me. It was stopping me from seeking God in prayer and through praise. I would wake up being suffocated in my sleep many nights, as if something was wrapped around my neck. The python spirit or girl possessed with a spirit of divination in Acts 16:16 was trying to distract Paul from prayer. She was really trying to stop him from his mission. The python spirit was trying to stop me from God's divine mission for my life. Paul delivered that young lady of the spirit, and he and Silas were put in bondage. While confined, they fought against this wickedness through prayer and praise.

I thank God, I was delivered of this spirit. I attended a prophetic conference to continue to gain wisdom and knowledge on how to operate in my calling. During the conference, there was praise, worship, and great teaching. After the first few speakers provided us with their lesson, an apostle held a deliverance service. She was walking throughout the area healing and setting people free. She called me to come to her, and I did with hesitation. Sometimes, we fear the unknown. When I walked up to her, she hit my back in several spots, and wasted no time to command the python spirit in the name of Jesus to be released off me. Immediately, I felt a power lift my hands up like there was a release, I let out a loud scream and bent over. I was set free!

Next, my continuous acts of sexual sin opened doors for the spirit of perversion, soul ties, and an incubus/succubus spirit. The spirit of perversion has so many different manifestations. I could have opened the door through my years of fornication, adultery, acts of sexual perversion, or abortions. During the night, I was being tormented in my sleep by sexual soul ties. My soul was tied to people I was giving life to, and so I was plagued with sexual dreams. Soul ties are formed when one person's soul is linked to the other person. That's why it's so common for women to not be with a person for 20 years, and they still have feelings for them. Soul ties are not formed only through sex though.

You can form a soul tie through a close relationship such as Jonathan and David in 1 Samuel 18:1, which states, "The soul of Jonathan was knit with the soul of David, and Jonathan loved him as his own soul." My soul had become tied to people through sexual intercourse. It was my desire to fornicate that caused me to become one with another person. 1 Corinthians 6:16 states, "What? Know ye not that he which is joined to an harlot is one body? For two, saith he, shall be one flesh." In my case, the linkage of our souls produced negative results. A demonic door was opened for the incubus/succubus spirit to attack. I had spiritual entities attacking me in my sleep having sexual intercourse with me. My husband would wake me up during the night because he knew something was not right, and he was correct.

Other things that were happening while I slept was I started seeing ancient creatures. Each dream showed a different family member that was dead. I learned if I communicated with these entities, I was opening a door to a demonic influence. From one of my dreams, the ancient creatures were trying to attack me. I was frightened, so I jumped out of my sleep fearful. It felt so real. The truth is these dreams are real. God showed me how I allowed an ancestral generational spirit access into my life. I knew every spirit that was attacking me. I started following apostles or pastors that operated in deliverance to see what actions I needed to take.

    I attended a cast out webinar that provided me information, but I was still being tormented. I continued to pray that God cleanse me from the things keeping me from being closer to Him. I knew I needed healing and restoration, and I was not the type that was afraid to admit it. One day, I ended up going to a conference for prophets. There was an apostle in the service who operated in deliverance. She ended up seeing the spiritual entities I was being oppressed by in the spiritual realm. She cast those spirits out of me that day. I remember being on the ground screaming uncontrollably while spitting up phlegm.

    If you have operated in deliverance, you know what I am talking about. I felt like I had cried for hours. I was full of a lot of feelings and emotions. I was thankful for deliverance, but I was upset I had to endure those things for that long. I had been carrying these spiritual entities for years. I went through a mourning phase for about two days until I heard the Spirit of God. He told me. "I gave you deliverance when I knew you were ready." The passage that came to my spirit after I received deliverance was when Jesus delivered the demon-possessed man (Mark chapter 5). After the man was delivered, Jesus told him to tell the people how great and compassionate God was.

I have learned instead of being shameful or embarrassed about being delivered, I am going to tell the whole world about the goodness of God. These are a few things I have overcome over the last few years. I was set free from my sins, and I was thankful. If we are not careful, we will continue to open doors for the enemy to gain access into our life. His access must be denied. This is real life people. I am not trying to scare anyone by sharing my testimony of the spirits I was oppressed with. I want people to understand these demonic powers exist. Demonic powers can enter your life at a young age and remain dormant for years. They will wait on the opportune time to attack.

If you continue to perform ungodly actions, there will be a consequence. I want you to understand if you continue to sin, or do not get delivered of your sins, you will give Satan access to your life. Do not allow Satan to operate in your life under any circumstance. You might think telling a little lie is harmless, but it is not. If you give him an inch, he will take a foot, then a yard. Cut off the access and seek God for your deliverance. I am thankful that I have been set free, and I will continue to seek God.

Your Choice, Your Sin

How was sin still affecting me if I gave my life to Christ? How can we overcome sin? I had to get delivered completely from things causing me to sin. There is no one on earth that can make you believe they are without sin. I am not saying it is impossible to be perfect if we strive to be like Christ. We can strive to become perfect beings, but again, it is a process. The Word of God tells us in 1 John 1:7-9, "if we say we have no sin, we deceive ourselves, and the truth is not within us. If we confess our sins, God is faithful and just to forgive us our sins and cleanse us from all unrighteousness."

Sin places a barrier between us and God. The persistent love of God allows us to receive redemption and forgiveness for our past, present, and future sins. When we decide to return to God, we receive a restoration of spiritual life. Our intimacy with God improves, our purpose is promising, and we chase after holiness, righteousness, and godliness. The grace and mercy of God provides restoration, and forgiveness gives us the ability to draw closer to God. I want to share a quick understanding of grace, mercy and forgiveness.

Grace is the unmerited favor of God. Mercy is the compassion or forgiveness an individual is given even though they should be punished. Forgiveness is when someone lets it go or gives us a pardon. For instance, a teenager becomes irate with their parents. The teenager begins to punch holes into the wall of her room. The parents forgive the teenager since they love her. They are compassionate even though there will still be consequences for her action. They make her fix the wall by telling her to patch it and paint it. As she is working hard to get the task done, they see the effort she is making and begin to help.

God provides favor when unexpected doors open in our lives. When we repent, God forgives us when we sin, but there will be consequences. The only difference is, because of His compassion, He gives us help even though we were guilty. He helps get us out of our mess. As a believer, I had to repent and confess my sins to God. A believer of God cannot be demon-possessed because their spirit belongs to God. The believer can be oppressed or tormented by demons, which is translated as demonization.

Demonic oppression is when Satan uses spiritual forces or entities to urge us to sin. He tries to convince us to deny God's Word. Satan's desire is for us to become spiritually dead, so we can be held in the bondage of sinful things. These negative influences affect the believer's life in some type of way. Do not believe every negative thing that happens in your life is demonic oppression. There could be other physical things happening in your life to cause problems. For instance, just because you have a continuous headache doesn't mean there is a spirit behind it. You will need to discern what is taking place. Demonic oppression can be viewed in several different ways according to the Word of God.

In Mark 5 and Luke 8, the man was fully owned or controlled by the devil. In Acts 5, Ananias and Sapphira hearts were filled by Satan. This heart issue these two had cost them their lives. Demon oppression can be the cause of a sickness or infirmity according to Luke 13:11,

Matthew 9:32, and Acts 19:16. As mentioned earlier, some sicknesses could be caused by a natural infirmity and at other times a demonic oppression. In Luke 13:10-13, the woman was bound by a spirit, a demon of infirmity, who afflicted her physical body for eighteen years causing her to bend over. The spirit of discernment enabled Jesus to reveal the presence of her spiritual affliction. Jesus took power and authority over the spirit. When Jesus was done speaking, he touched her, and she was set free and her body straightened up.

The woman was delivered from the demon, but Jesus still had to touch her to heal her physical infirmity. Jesus, having the ability to discern the spirit delivered this woman from a demon that caused a physical infirmity. If you're having an issue that won't go away, I suggest you seek medical attention. When you seek medical attention and no test or examination can reveal the problem, you might be dealing with a higher presence. I suggest you consult with spiritual counsel who operate in deliverance ministry. They will discern what is taking place and use their power and authority to cast the spirit out. Demonic oppression occurs, but the power of God has authority over the enemy.

The work Jesus Christ performed on the cross is the only power we need to become victorious over the enemy. In Mark 1:27, Jesus commanded the unclean spirits to obey him. Colossians 2:15 states, "Having disarmed the powers and authorities, he made a public spectacle of them, triumphing over them by the cross" (NIV). We must understand Jesus seats above every demonic power to destroy the work of Satan. It is the power and authority of Jesus that we need. By grace, we have been given the power and authority over the army of Satan. Our power does not come from us, it comes from Christ. Demons can attack believers of God, but we have power and authority over them. "I have given you authority to trample on snakes and scorpions and to overcome all the power of the enemy; nothing will harm you" (Luke 10:19, NIV). Victory belongs to Jesus!

Questions for Reflection

1) How can you locate the source where you have given Satan a foothold in your life?

2) What does it mean to you to be truly delivered? Have you been delivered?

3) Do you believe the power and authority of Christ has been given to you? Why?

Chapter 9
God Changed my Name

There is a name above every name, and that name is Jesus Christ. When I started dating my husband in Hawaii, we became great friends and lovers. He had one child, which was a little boy, and I had two children. We deployed back to Iraq a year later, and during the deployment he decided to propose. I never knew love could feel so great until I met him. We were married that year while on vacation from the deployment. I could see the road at the end of the tunnel until my new husband wanted to have children. For some reason, I could not get pregnant. I pondered on the previous abortions and began to think I would never give my husband a child.

One day, my supervisor provided me with words of encouragement. He told me the devil could not stop me from having children. He instructed me to ask God for forgiveness and pray for a child. That night, I did what I was told. I learned I was pregnant a few months later before we returned from the deployment. This is what happens when we trust God. God opens the floodgates of heaven and pours out a blessing we do not have room enough to receive. My husband and I ended up having three girls together.

My life started to have purpose. I had a wonderful husband and children that loved me. One principle we desired to keep in our blended family was our faith in God. Although our faith was tested plenty of times, we never gave up. My husband told me, he desired change in his life because he saw the way God was working in me. This motivated me to be a woman chasing after God's heart. I had to provide a perfect example of a virtuous woman for my daughters.

I decided to rededicate my life to Christ and allow the Holy Spirit to be my spiritual guide. When the power of Jesus is released in someone's life, He takes up occupancy in the vessel. He washes away our sins and adds our name to the Lamb's Book of Life. I changed from a person who once looked in a mirror and saw a distorted image to a person who had purpose. I saw the calling and anointing God placed in my life instead of my sins. The vision God provided was distorted because I wore my sins not understanding the purpose of Jesus Christ. Jesus died for every person to have life. A life of purpose without sin. There is no sin that can hide from the name of Jesus. It's discouraging to know the Word of God but allow your sins to stop you from living a life of greatness.

Knowing who I was in God was my motivation to walk into my God-given purpose. When you know the power and authority you walk in as a believer, you do not focus on the naysayers. Those people are sent as distractions. As I changed my name, my husband took notice. Our lives started slowly transforming for the better. He changed from a person who had gold teeth in his mouth, sagged his pants, and used inappropriate and profane language. I watched God clean him up day-by-day, but it was a process. My husband and my oldest son were baptized on the same day. I was a very proud wife and mother. My husband became an example of what a man of God is supposed to be for our children, and husband for me.

When you adjust your vision, you can see a once blurred image more clearly. Standing in the mirror now shows the perfect creation God made in me. My husband says I look in the mirror too much now. I probably do, but I know I do not look like what I have been through. As a mental health professional, who deals with people who cannot see the God within them, I tell them to keep Scriptural truths by their mirror.

When they feel hopeless or want to give up, they can remember the promises God made. Some examples include: I am fearfully and wonderfully made; made in the image of God; He's the potter and I am the clay; far above rubies; blessed in the city and in the fields; adopted into the family of God. Declare with me, "the devil cannot distort my vision or steal my purpose. I am who God says that I am." My name has been changed! I have been given a new identity in Christ.

Questions for Reflection

1) Have you given your life to Christ? Has your name been added to the Lamb's Book of Life?

2) What is your new identity that Christ has established?

3) What steps will you take to revert to your old self? What is your new mission in God?

Chapter 10
Write the Vision, Make it Plain

Imagine being in a marriage where one spouse is looking for a job. They haven't worked in about a year. Every day they go without a job, you stress yourself out. Daily, your significant other takes the initiative to dress up, put in applications and interview for positions. Even though they're putting forth effort, you become discouraged and start thinking irrationally. Your significant other tries to calm you and assure you, but you don't listen. You're so overwhelmed with this issue you start problems in your marriage. You can't be patient and wait on the Lord. Now, you're struggling with unnecessary anxiety and uncertainty.

My grandmother Ruth told me to stop searching for tomorrow and live for today. She explained that everyone was living their lives worrying about what they can do for tomorrow. They lose focus on what they can do for today. People have lost focus on the present. The Word of God tells us not to worry about tomorrow. Tomorrow will worry about itself. Each day carries its own problems. I know people want to be prepared but worrying about tomorrow will only add to the emotional load. Instead of worrying about your spouse not having a job, provide that person with words of affirmation that will encourage them. Beating that person down with your words and worrying will not help. It will only affect both of your emotions.

One way to stop worrying about tomorrow is to create a plan. You do not have to wait for things to happen. Having a plan prepares you for the future without causing emotional turmoil. A person that plans, prepares action steps to achieve a specific goal. Some people think a plan is just like a map. A plan will identify how far you progressed toward your goal, and how far you must go to reach your destination. When you create a plan, you will learn to stop worrying about unnecessary things. I host vision board workshops through my business to enable clients to write their vision down on a poster. The vision board can consist of your godly vision and a personal vision.

This project captures your vision, dreams, hopes and desires. It's a visual and written representation which inspires change and encourages you to progress. I created my vision board for this year. I focused on the vision God gave me and the goals I had for myself. I believe everything I placed on my vision board is God's purpose for my life. If God said it, it will come to pass. Creating a vision board is a great way to not focus on tomorrow because you believe your vision will come to pass. When creating the vision board, you are trusting in God to order your steps. I love when I see things happening in my life that is placed on my vision board. It reminds me God has a plan for my life, and I am living my purpose.

Questions for Reflection

1) How many times have you focused on the problems of tomorrow?

2) What have you done with the vision God has given you?

3) What necessary steps do you take to write the vision down?

Chapter 11
Walking in my God-Given Purpose

Serving God became a faith walk for me. When I became obedient to God, I was given a glimpse of my purpose. It is important to distinguish between God's vision and a personal vision. A godly vision is a divine revelation or prophetic insight given from God. The revelation can be given directly from God, or by one of His messengers. Ultimately, our blueprint for our lives was placed within our heart. Ecclesiastes 3:11 states, "He has also set eternity in the human heart; yet no one can fathom what God has done from beginning to end" (NIV). God's plans for us have already been laid out for eternity (Ecclesiastes 3:15, 6:10). Everything is already decided, we must seek God for the plan.

A personal vision is created by you and focuses on your career success, relationships, and overall satisfaction for your life. A personal vision will express your sense of purpose and meaning of life. It is critical to align our life according to God's vision. It is not a bad idea to create a personal vision, but it is God's vision that will determine your purpose. I write down every vision God gives me. God releases His word to me through dreams, visions, miracles, signs, and prophetic words. I started understanding the words of Jeremiah 29:11, which states "For I know the plans I have for you, declares the Lord, plans to prosper you and not to harm you, plans to give you hope and a future."

Knowing this passage, I cannot let the devil, or my past hold me back from God's promises. Following after God is like running a race. You cannot give up and you must condition your body to endure. Even though other people are on the track competing against you, you must keep your eyes on the finish line (God). Stop looking back on your past sins. Change your focus to God's promises for your life. Remember anything that goes against the Word of God is of the devil. Sometimes, I look back at my past to measure how far I've come. I will state my accomplishments here, not to brag on myself, but to boast about the glory of God.

I have been married to my wonderful husband for nine years, but we have been in a relationship for eleven years. People prophesied we would be pastors who shared their wisdom to other marriages and families. Although, we did not believe the word then, that vision is starting to come to fruition. One day, I attended the education center to find a degree program for my master's degree. I wanted to become a social worker due to a tragedy one of my family members faced in her life. When I started talking to the Education Specialist, he directed me towards Liberty University.

I applied to a Christian university that offered a marriage and family degree. I did not think God wanted me to become a marriage and family therapist since I had a previous divorce, but I was wrong. I started my educational journey for my graduate degree that day, and God continues to reveal my purpose. God showed me He would use my imperfections to make me a great counselor. Honestly, my transparency in counseling has allowed my clients to see the light in their dark world.

I am a mother of six talented children who serve God with their whole hearts.

I pray the blessings of God over their lives, so they do not have to experience the pain and suffering I endured. My husband and I trained them up in God, so they will understand where their help comes from. My oldest son ministers, praise dances, and raps through spoken word. I understand why God would not allow me to get rid of such a precious jewel. Watching his love for God is such a blessing. My oldest daughter praise dances and models.

When she is walking that runway, I can see the grace of God on her life. My other son praise dances as well. At first, he was skeptical, but one of our pastors asked him to dance, and he has been dancing ever since. The three little ones I have with my husband are very special in their own way. Their knowledge of the Word of God and their ability to use wisdom is profound at their age. They amaze me every day.

Through work, God blessed me to receive an early retirement from the military. I thank God for the experiences I had in the military, which provided me stability and a foundation for my family. The Army afforded me with a great education. I finished a Bachelor of Arts degree in Social Science from Ashford University, and a Master of Arts degree in Marriage and Family Therapy from Liberty University.

I hope to become licensed in Alabama within the next few years. One day, I will own and operate a counseling center. Currently, I'm pursuing a Graduate Certificate of Completion in Life Coaching from Grand Canyon University. Also, I want to become a Certified Family Life Educator and provide education to families through various services. But, I will take one day at a time.

I currently work for a foster care organization that focuses on preserving families and securing futures. The organization provides preservation and reunification services to families that need assistance. Our job as professionals is to teach families skills and techniques needed to become effective parents. Also, we provide therapy to address their problems and change their behavior and thinking.

My husband and my transformation renewed our minds and changed our lives. We surrendered our lives to Christ and decided to serve Him with our whole heart. Following God will not be easy. We have separated ourselves from a lot of people, places, and things. Sometimes, we left kicking and screaming, but God knew best. Separation is good when God is taking you to places of great responsibility and authority. We know the calling on our lives, and the things God desires for us to do. Every day is a struggle, but you must keep the faith. I promise the blessings of God are well worth it, especially receiving eternal rewards.

My husband and I have started The Center of Empowerment, a family-owned establishment that focuses on the WHOLE (mind, body, spirit, and soul) you. My husband is the owner and operator of the Spirit of Life Fitness LLC, which is a fitness training practice that specializes in spiritual health and fitness. I'm the owner and operator of Empowering Visions, LLC, which is a life coaching practice that specializes in spiritual health and wellness. I became a Certified Professional Life Coach (CPLC) with a Christian niche through New Life Coach, Inc. This organization enabled me to share the Gospel while helping people remove the barriers in their lives.

I started hosting empowerment conferences and workshops, and I have been asked to speak at engagements. Through the business, we empower, inspire and encourage people of God to walk into their God-given purpose. I view myself as a transformational coach because when I speak, the glory of God comes out my mouth.

The Word of God has the power to transform people. I utilize my personal experiences and prophetic ministry to evangelize to God's people. The business enables me to sell my books, Christian apparel, life coaching sessions, and be an inspirational speaker. I am about to start hosting empowerment calls monthly, and coffee and conversation engagements quarterly. On August 1, 2018, I will be launching the Empowerment Academy, which is an online learning academy for teen empowerment. This online academy will provide a Christian Education program. There will be different courses offered each month for a small fee. Eventually, I will add courses to empower marriages and families.

My assignment is to focus on teenagers right now. It is all about empowering people to come out of their dark places into the light of God. He is the way, truth, and the light. I do not want people to just exist in life. I want people to start living a purposeful life. I am thankful God has provided me a platform to reach the nations. I think being an author and telling my story, transformation, and understanding of God is a blessing. I get to share this information through teaching, preaching, and books. There is no greater feeling than living a life of purpose.

When I think about the person I used to be, I thank God for change. It is crazy how distorted the enemy had my vision. To look in the mirror and only see your mistakes is not motivating. Actually, it was pretty discouraging. My vision is clear now, and I live out my purpose daily. God is trying to birth so many great things out of me, I just have to learn humility and patience. Right now, I throw my hands up and surrender to His will. I am living out my purpose on purpose. Ultimately, my job is to save souls for the Kingdom of God.

Questions for Reflection

1) What is your life purpose?

2) Are you ready to walk out your God-given purpose?

3) Will you function at your full potential? Why?

4) What will it take to become successful in God?

The Author's Final Words

I am so very grateful God chose me to write this book. I want to leave some godly wisdom with you before you finish. Psalm 23:4 states, "Even though I walk through the darkest valley, I will fear no evil, for you are with me; your rod and your staff, they comfort me." I feel like I have walked in a few valley's most of my life. A valley is a low-lying area of land that is positioned between hills or mountains. It is a landform that became sunken or depressed below the surrounding area. A valley is depicted as a place of darkness, a dark shadow, or the shadow of death.

In the Bible, mountains or hills are symbolic to people believing they were "closer to God" who dwelled in the heavens. God often revealed himself to people on the mountaintop. Psalm 72:3 describes the mountains as bringing prosperity to the people, and the hills the fruit of righteousness. When I hear of mountaintops and hills, I think of blessings, and a valley reminds me of destruction. The valley became a place of danger. David, in this psalm, is telling us he has walked in the darkest valley, but he was not afraid. Most of us will have to walk through a valley to get to our purpose. Walking through the valley is not the problem, the problem occurs when we decide to stay in the sunken place.

We have all been to valley places. If not, prepare to go. See, Ezekiel was taken to the middle of a valley by the Spirit of God. He found a place full of bones in that valley. It was a place where people traveled to, became stuck, but did not walk through. They ended up staying there. Their problems in their mind were too great. Maybe their children were not listening, and they gave up. The job they worked for twenty years dissatisfied them. Their marriage began falling apart. They were overwhelmed with paying bills. They experienced the death of a family member and could not stop grieving. Maybe anxiety and depression set in their life, and they felt hopeless or helpless.

These are real-life situations people endure on a daily basis which lead them to their valley places. David referred to the valley as the "shadow of death." Sometimes, it is hard to navigate through life when you are faced with problems all around you. It might seem like you are on your death bed. Many of us focus on the problem without putting our faith in God. God directed Ezekiel to bring those dry bones back to life. God wanted Ezekiel to revive Israel. God made the impossible seem possible. He wanted Ezekiel to prophesy or speak to those dry bones using the Word of God.

God had the power to help and restore what was lost. We will face difficult times in our lives and it might seem like the situation will not get better, but you must bring life to your valley experiences. When you face trials, trust God. When you feel discouraged, trust God. When you make a mistake, and want to give up, trust God. The power of God can resurrect us out of those dark places, out of the valley. The first step I will leave with you is when entering your valley, continue to walk. Do not stop and become complacent with life. I have never experienced a trial that God brought me into and did not bring me out. He will provide the necessary steps or guidance needed to get through.

Next step, remember it is just a shadow. A shadow is an area of darkness that is created when a source of light is blocked. When you are in the shadow, understand your view is just blocked. The shadow is temporary. My son is way taller than me. Normally, I stand right in his shadow to hide from the sun. The thing I have learned is if I move to the left or right of his shadow, I move into the path of the sun. Listen, if you change your direction or move out of the shadow, the light is still shining. Only light can drive out darkness. The way you move out of the shadow is by recognizing what you are dealing with. Admit you have a problem and allow God to help you. You must look past your problem and realize your purpose is still there.

Lastly, if you continue to walk, and move out of your shadow, you will realize God was with you the whole time. David said he was not afraid because God was with him in the valley. God carried the rod and staff. The rod was for protection, and staff for direction. God kept David from fearing, provided him protection and direction, and comforted him. God is our refuge. He is the shelter we run to when faced with danger or trouble. Run to Him to provide strength and hope during your times of trouble. God can bring us out of every difficulty and trial.

Appendix A
Practical Exercise

Practical Exercise 1

Use this section to write down the sins that have your vision distorted. Take your time and be careful to list each one. Pray over these sins and ask God to forgive you. Do not allow your vision to become distorted by looking back on them.

_____

_____

_____

_____

_____

_____

_____

_____

Practical Exercise 2

Write down your testimony as a story. This part should be easy since you already listed your sins on the previous exercise. Use your testimony as a conversion story for others. Pull out main concepts from your story to make it easier. People want to hear your testimony, so learn to share it when given the opportunity to minister to lost souls.

_____

_____

_____

_____

_____

_____

_____

_____

Practical Exercise 3

What broken pieces exist in your life that you desire God to put back together? Write these things down on a sheet of paper. Lift these things up to God in prayer. Ask God to give you ways to fill the spaces.

_____

_____

_____

_____

_____

_____

_____

Practical Exercise 4

Grab a mirror from around your house or from a dollar store. I want you to look in the mirror at God's wonderful creation. As you look in the mirror, write down a list of things God attributes to you or prophetic words you have received from others through the spirit. A few things God said about me was I was called as a prophet, so I wrote that on my mirror. You can use Scriptures and place it on the mirror. For instance, the Word of God declares you are fearfully and wonderfully made. You can write that message on the mirror. Use these valuable words and phrases when needed for encouragement. Do not discard the mirror!

_____

_____

_____

_____

_____

_____

_____

_____

Practical Exercise 5

Create a godly vision for your life. Create a personal vision for your life. Seek God through prayer and fasting, silence and solitude, and reading and meditating on the Word of God to provide you with a vision. What vision did God provide you? What vision did you provide for yourself? How does your vision relate to your purpose?

_____

_____

_____

_____

_____

_____

_____

Practical Exercise 6

Use the vision you created, God's vision and create a vision board. Supplies needed: poster board, glue or glue stick, scissor, markers, and magazines. Before you begin, pray and ask God to give you revelation. Next, take time and think about your dreams or goals. Create your vision board as a collage. Cut out pictures or words for your spiritual journey, ministry, where you would like to travel, places you would like to go, things you would like to do, personal development, your educational journey and career, health and fitness, finances, and what you desire for your relationship and family. Use your creativity and glue the things on there. Pray over your vision board and post it somewhere in your home where it is noticeable. Make sure to look at your vision every week. Believe in your vision, and watch it come to pass.

Practical Exercise 7

Seven is the foundation of God's word; it represents the number of completion and divine perfection (both physical and spiritual). Remember, God created so many great things in seven days. On the seventh exercise, I want you to focus on every goal you have envisioned. Write a plan to accomplish each goal. The planning process enables you to create a course of action to achieve a goal. During the planning process, you can review, identify, and improve anything that needs to be refined. Planning allows you to envision your results and determine the steps necessary to reach your destination. Set the goal, formulate a plan, and put it into action!

Appendix B
Cognitive Distortions

List of Cognitive Distortions

In this section, I will list the common cognitive distortions people are faced with according to the psychology field. The information used in this section is taken from Dr. John M. Grohol *Psych Central* article, "15 Common Cognitive Distortions" (https://psychcentral.com/lib/15-common-cognitive-distortions/). Psychologist Aaron Beck first proposed the theory behind cognitive distortions in 1976, and in the 1980s, David Burns popularized it. A cognitive distortion is when our mind tries to convince us of something that isn't true. A cognitive distortion produces inaccurate thoughts that support negative thinking or emotions. Our mind tells us things that sound rational and accurate, but truthfully, it keeps us feeling bad about ourselves. You must correctly identify cognitive distortions, not answer negative thoughts back, and refute them. Refuting negative thinking will help diminish the distortions. The cognitive distortions are as follows:

Filtering: we take the negative details and magnify them while filtering out all positive aspects of a situation.

Polarized Thinking (Black and White Thinking): we believe something is either black or white. We must be perfect or we're a failure, there is no middle ground.

Overgeneralization: we come to a general conclusion based on a single incident or a single piece of evidence. Something bad can happen once, and we believe it will happen repeatedly.

Jumping to Conclusions: without individuals saying so, we know what they are feeling and why they act the way they do. We determine how people are feeling toward us.

Catastrophizing: we expect disaster to strike, no matter what. This is also referred to as "magnifying or minimizing." We hear about a problem and use what if questions.

Personalization: a person believes everything others do or say is a direct, personal reaction to the person. We also compare ourselves to others, trying to determine who is smarter or better looking.

Control Fallacies: if we feel externally controlled, we see ourselves as helpless victims of fate. The fallacy of internal control has us assuming responsibility for the pain and happiness of everyone around us.

Fallacy of Fairness: we feel resentful because we think we know what is fair, but other people won't agree with us.

Blaming: we hold other people responsible for our pain or take the other track and blame ourselves for every problem.

Should's: we have a list of ironclad rules about how others and ourselves should behave. A person may often believe they are trying to motivate themselves with *should* and *shouldn't's*, as if they must be punished before they can do anything.

Emotional Reasoning: we believe that what we feel must be true automatically. You assume that your unhealthy emotions reflect the way things really are.

Fallacy of Change: we expect that other people will change to suit us if we just pressure or cajole them enough. We need to change people because our hopes for happiness seem to depend entirely on them.

Global Labeling: we generalize one or two qualities into a negative global judgment. These are extreme forms of generalizing and are also referred to as "labeling" and "mislabeling." Instead of describing an error in context of a specific situation, a person will attach an unhealthy label to themselves.

Always Being Right: we are continually on trial to prove that our opinions and actions are correct. Being wrong is unthinkable and we will go to any length to demonstrate our rightness.

Heaven's Reward Fallacy: we expect our sacrifice and self-denial to pay off, as if someone is keeping score. We feel bitter when the reward doesn't come.

About the Author

Jennifer Marion is a licensed minister and native of Gulfport, MS. She is the daughter of Toney Ferrill, Sr., and Joann Neely. She entered the United States Army in April 2002, where she met and married her husband of eight years, Minister Earlmondish Marion. They have six children, Jayshon, Ayana, Earl Jr., Jayden, Jenesis, and Erin. Jennifer's husband separated from the military in August 2017, while she retired from the military in August 2017. They currently reside in Madison, Alabama.

Jennifer had a passion to write from an early age. Her grandmother Ruth inspired her to pick up the pen and start writing. She decided to chase after her dreams and become an inspiration to others through her writing. The Holy Spirit revealed to her what she needed to write down. Through her writing, she evangelizes and empowers people to walk into their God-given purpose. She is a teacher of the Word of God; her focus is on reaching lost souls for the kingdom of God. As a visionary leader, she communicates the will of God through personal experiences and prophetic ministry.

An avid scholar, Jennifer finished her Bachelor of Arts in Social Science from Ashford University. She decided to pursue her Master of Arts in Marriage and Family Therapy from Liberty University. She is currently pursuing a Graduate Certificate of Completion in Life Coaching from Grand Canyon University. She is a Certified Professional Life Coach (CPLC) with a Christian niche from New Life Coach Inc. She is the Owner and Founder of Empowering Visions, LLC, a Christian-based, life coaching practice that inspires people to achieve greatness in their lives. It is designed to help others develop a strong sense of self and create and maintain a balanced lifestyle.

Jennifer offers vision board workshops, life skill classes and training, empowerment seminars and workshops, spiritual warfare training, and conferences. She is an empowerment coach, inspirational leader, and Christian author. She has published three other books to date. *Graced for This* and *Empowering Visions* is currently available through Xulon Press, Amazon, and Barnes & Noble. *40 Days of Empowerment* is available through Manifested Truth Publishing, her business website, and Amazon. For a personal autographed copy, and to reserve Empowering Visions, LLC, for a speaking engagement, visit her website at http://www.empoweringvisions05.com.

Contact Information and Social Media:
Contact her by email: empoweringvisions05@gmail.com
Follow her on Facebook: Jennifer Ann Marion (mz.jennmarion)
Business page on FB: Empowering Visions, LLC (empoweringvisons05)
Twitter: (@jennymarion05)
Instagram: (@jennymarion05)

Additional Author Publications

"Graced for This"

A story about God's amazing grace. This book provides scriptural truth and understanding of the transformation of a sinner to a Saint. God is calling His people to get off the pew and start being a servant to the kingdom of God. Are you graced for the journey ahead?

ISBN 978-1-4984-7486-3 **138 pages**

Graced for This can be purchased through the Xulon Press Bookstore, Amazon, and Barnes and Noble. Grab your copy today!

"Empowering Visions"

Discover the vision God has for your life. How would your life change if you discovered your purpose for the kingdom of God? In *Empowering Visions*, Jennifer Marion enlightens you on how to acquire God's direction. God has provided all His children with purpose. Your purpose is embedded within your heart. It's up to you to discover yourself.

ISBN 978-1-5456-2050-2 **146 pages**

Empowering Visions can be purchased through the Xulon Press Bookstore, Amazon, and Barnes and Noble. Get your copy today!

"40 Days of Empowerment"

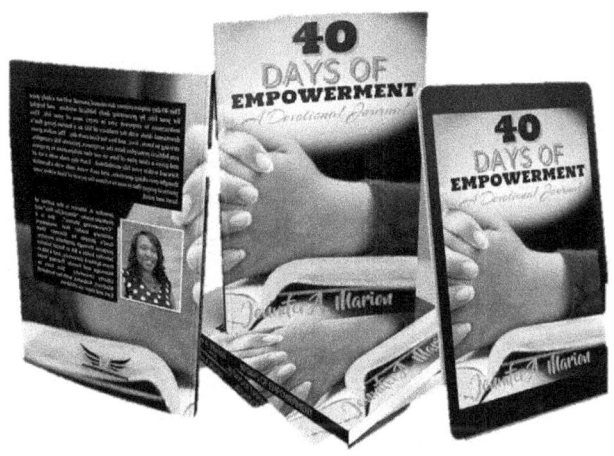

This devotional journal will set a daily pace for your life; by presenting biblical wisdom and principles, scriptures, present life examples, and helpful instructions to empower you in every area of your life. It deals with the realities of life as a human being that's striving to know, love, and live for God each day.

ISBN 978-0578202181 216 **pages**

40 Days of Empowerment can be purchased through the author's website, Manifested Truth Publishing, and Amazon. Get your copy today!

www.ingramcontent.com/pod-product-compliance
Lightning Source LLC
Chambersburg PA
CBHW071200090426
42736CB00012B/2392